CIH CERTIFIED INCIDENT HANDLER V2 EXAM PREP AND DUMPS

Exam Study Materials for EC-Council

Published by:

Impact Books

Cover & Interior Designed By

By

Sharon Loxley

1st Edition

Impact Books: Empowering Minds, Changing Lives

At Impact Books, we believe in the transformative power of knowledge. We are not just a publisher; we are a catalyst for change, a platform that empowers minds, and a gateway to new perspectives. Our mission is to bring impactful non-fiction literature to the world, shaping lives and fostering growth through the written word.

Our journey began with a small team of dedicated individuals

who shared a common dream: to provide a voice for writers whose stories and expertise could inspire and educate. Over the years,

we have grown into a diverse family of authors, editors, designers, and collaborators united by our commitment to quality, integrity, and making a positive impact on readers worldwide.

QUESTION 1

Which of the following terms may be defined as "a measure of possible inability to achieve a goal, objective, or target within a defined security, cost plan and technical limitations that adversely affects the organization's operation and revenues?

A. Risk
B. Vulnerability
C. Threat
D. Incident Response

QUESTION 2

A distributed Denial of Service (DDoS) attack is a more common type of DoS Attack, where a single system is targeted by a large number of infected machines over the Internet. In a DDoS attack, attackers first infect multiple systems which are known as:

A. Trojans
B. Zombies
C. C. Spyware
C. Worms

QUESTION 3

The goal of incident response is to handle the incident in a way that minimizes damage and reduces recovery time and cost. Which of the following does **NOT** constitute a goal of incident response?

A. Dealing with human resources department and various employee conflict behaviors.

B. Using information gathered during incident handling to prepare for handling future incidents in a better way and to provide stronger protection for systems and data.

C. Helping personal to recover quickly and efficiently from security incidents, minimizing loss or theft and disruption of services.

D. Dealing properly with legal issues that may arise during incidents.

QUESTION 4

An organization faced an information security incident where a disgruntled employee passed sensitive access control information to a competitor. The organization's incident response manager, upon investigation, found that the incident must be handled within a few hours on the same day to maintain business continuity and market competitiveness. How would you categorize such information security incident?

A. High level incident
B. Middle level incident
C. Ultra-High level incident
D. Low level incident

QUESTION 5

Business continuity is defined as the ability of an organization to continue to function even after a disastrous event, accomplished through the deployment of redundant hardware and software, the use of fault tolerant systems, as well as a solid backup and recovery strategy. Identify the plan which is mandatory part of a business continuity plan?

A. Forensics Procedure Plan
B. Business Recovery Plan
C. Sales and Marketing plan
D. New business strategy plan

QUESTION 6

The flow chart gives a view of different roles played

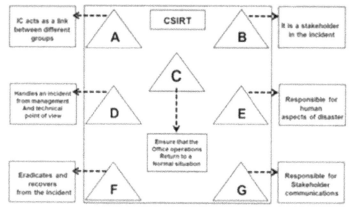

by the different personnel of CSIRT. Identify the incident response personnel denoted by A, B, C, D, E, F and G.

A. A-Incident Analyst, B- Incident Coordinator, C-Public Relations, D-Administrator, E- Human Resource, F-Constituency, G-Incident Manager

B. A- Incident Coordinator, B-Incident Analyst, C-Public Relations, D-Administrator, E- Human Resource, F-Constituency, G-Incident ManagerC. A- Incident Coordinator, B- Constituency, C-Administrator, D-Incident Manager, E- Human Resource, F-Incident Analyst, G-Public relations

C. A- Incident Manager, B-Incident Analyst, C-Public Relations, D-Administrator, E- Human Resource, F-Constituency, G-Incident Coordinator

QUESTION 7 Which of the following is an appropriate flow of the incident recovery steps?

A. System Operation-System Restoration-System Validation-System Monitoring
B. System Validation-System Operation-System Restoration-System Monitoring
C. System Restoration-System Monitoring-System Validation-System Operations
D. System Restoration-System Validation-System Operations-System Monitoring

QUESTION 8
A computer Risk Policy is a set of ideas to be implemented to overcome the risk associated with computer security incidents. Identify the procedure that is **NOT** part of the computer risk policy?

A. Procedure to identify security funds to hedge risk
B. Procedure to monitor the efficiency of security controls
C. Procedure for the ongoing training of employees authorized to access the system
D. Provisions for continuing support if there is an interruption in the system or if the system crashes

QUESTION 9

Identify the network security incident where intended authorized users are prevented from using system, network, or applications by flooding the network with high volume of traffic that consumes all existing network resources.

A. URL Manipulation
B. XSS Attack
C. SQL Injection
D. Denial of Service Attack

QUESTION 10

Incident handling and response steps help you to detect, identify, respond and manage an incident. Which of the following steps focus on limiting the scope and extent of an incident?

A. Eradication
B. Containment
C. Identification
D. Data collection

QUESTION 11

Identify the malicious program that is masked as a genuine harmless program and gives the attacker unrestricted access to the user's information and system. These programs may unleash dangerous programs that may erase the unsuspecting user's disk and send the victim's credit card numbers and passwords to a stranger.

A. Cookie tracker

B. Worm

C. Trojan

D. Virus

QUESTION 12

Quantitative risk is the numerical determination of the probability of an adverse event and the extent of the losses due to the event. Quantitative risk is calculated as:

A. (Probability of Loss) X (Loss)

B. (Loss) / (Probability of Loss)

C. (Probability of Loss) / (Loss)

D. Significant Risks X Probability of Loss X Loss

QUESTION 13

An incident recovery plan is a statement of actions that should be taken before, during or after an incident. Identify which of the following is **NOT** an objective of the incident recovery plan?

A. Creating new business processes to maintain profitability after incident
B. Providing a standard for testing the recovery plan
C. Avoiding the legal liabilities arising due to incident
D. Providing assurance that systems are reliable

QUESTION 14

Risk is defined as the probability of the occurrence of an incident. Risk formulation generally begins with the likeliness of an event's occurrence, the harm it may cause and is usually denoted as Risk = $\sum$(events)X(Probability of occurrence)X?

A. Magnitude
B. Probability
C. Consequences
D. Significance

QUESTION 15

An audit trail policy collects all audit trails such as series of records of computer events, about an operating system, application or user activities. Which of the following statements is **NOT** true for an audit trail policy:

A. It helps tracking individual actions and allows users to be personally accountable for their actions

B. It helps in compliance to various regulatory laws, rules,and guidelines

C. It helps in reconstructing the events after a problem has occurred

QUESTION 16

Computer forensics is methodical series of techniques and procedures for gathering evidence from computing equipment, various storage devices and or digital media that can be presented in a course of law in a coherent and meaningful format. Which one of the following is an appropriate flow of steps in the computer forensics process:

A. Examination> Analysis > Preparation > Collection > Reporting

B. Preparation > Analysis > Collection > Examination > Reporting

C. Analysis > Preparation > Collection > Reporting > Examination

D. Preparation > Collection > Examination > Analysis > Reporting

QUESTION 17

Multiple component incidents consist of a combination of two or more attacks in a system. Which of the following is not a multiple component incident?

A. An insider intentionally deleting files from a workstation

B. An attacker redirecting user to a malicious website and infects his system with Trojan

C. An attacker infecting a machine to launch a **DDoS** attack

D. An attacker using email with malicious code to infect internal workstation

QUESTION 18

Computer Forensics is the branch of forensic science in which legal evidence is found in any computer or any digital media device. Of the following, who is responsible for examining the evidence acquired and separating the useful evidence?

A. Evidence Supervisor

B. Evidence Documenter

C. Evidence Manager

D. Evidence Examiner/ Investigator

QUESTION 19 The network perimeter should be configured in such a way that it denies all incoming and outgoing traffic/ services that are not required. Which service listed below, if blocked, can help in preventing Denial of Service attack?

A. POP3 service

B. SMTP service

C. Echo service

QUESTION 20

A US Federal agency network was the target of a DoS attack that prevented and impaired the normal authorized functionality of the networks. According to agency's reporting timeframe guidelines, this incident should be reported within two

(2) HOURS of discovery/detection if the successful attack is still ongoing and the agency is unable to successfully mitigate the activity. Which incident category of the US Federal Agency does this incident belong to?

A.CAT 5

B.CAT 1

C. CAT 2

D. CAT 6

QUESTION 21 US-CERT and Federal civilian agencies use the reporting timeframe criteria in the federal agency reporting categorization. What is the timeframe required to report an incident under the CAT 4 Federal Agency category?

A. Weekly
B. Within four (4) hours of discovery/detection if the successful attack is still ongoing and agency is unable to successfully mitigate activity
C. Within two (2) hours of discovery/detection
D. Monthly

QUESTION 22

Identify a standard national process which establishes a set of activities, general tasks and a management structure to certify and accredit systems that will maintain the information assurance (IA) and security posture of a system or site.

A. NIASAP
B. NIAAAP
C. NIPACP
D. NIACAP

QUESTION 23 Policies are designed to protect the organizational resources on the network by establishing the set rules and procedures. Which of the following policies authorizes a group of users to perform a set of actions on a set of resources?

A. Access control policy
B. Audit trail policy
C. Logging policy
D. Documentation policy

QUESTION 24
When an employee is terminated from his or her job, what should be the next immediate step taken by an organization?

A. All access rights of the employee to physical locations, networks, systems, applications and data should be disabled
B. The organization should enforce separation of duties
C. The access requests granted to an employee should be documented and vetted by the supervisor
D. The organization should monitor the activities of the system administrators and privileged users who have permissions to access the sensitive information

QUESTION 25

A threat source does not present a risk if **NO** vulnerability that can be exercised for a particular threat source. Identify the step in which different threat sources are defined:

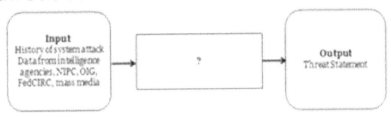

A. Identification Vulnerabilities

B. Control analysis

C. Threat identification

D. System characterization

QUESTION 26

In the Control Analysis stage of the NIST's risk assessment methodology, technical and none technical control methods are classified into two categories. What are these two control categories?

A. Preventive and Detective controls

B. Detective and Disguised controls

C. Predictive and Detective controls

D. Preventive and predictive controls

QUESTION 27

Which of the following incident recovery testing methods works by creating a mock disaster, like fire to identify the reaction of the procedures that are implemented to handle such situations?

A. Scenario testing
B. Facility testing
C. Live walk-through testing
D. Procedure testing

QUESTION 28

An incident is analyzed for its nature, intensity and its effects on the network and systems. Which stage of the incident response and handling process involves auditing the system and network log files?

A. Incident recording
B. Reporting
C. Containment
D. Identification

QUESTION 29

Which among the following CERTs is an Internet provider to higher education institutions and various other research institutions in the Netherlands and deals with all cases related to computer security incidents in which a customer is involved either as a victim or as a suspect?

A. NET-CERT
B. DFN-CERT
C. Funet CERT
D. SURFnet-CERT

QUESTION 30

One of the main objectives of incident management is to prevent incidents and attacks by tightening the physical security of the system or infrastructure. According to CERT's incident management process, which stage focuses on implementing infrastructure improvements resulting from postmortem reviews or other process improvement mechanisms?

A. Protection
B. Preparation
C. Detection
D. Triage

QUESTION 31

Risk management consists of three processes, risk assessment, mitigation and evaluation. Risk assessment determines the extent of the potential threat and the risk associated with an IT system through its SDLC. How many primary steps does NIST's risk assessment methodology involve?

A. Twelve
B. FourC. Six
C. Nine

QUESTION 32

Insider threats can be detected by observing concerning behaviors exhibited by insiders, such as conflicts with supervisors and coworkers, decline in performance, tardiness or unexplained absenteeism. Select the technique that helps in detecting insider threats:

A. Correlating known patterns of suspicious and malicious behavior
B. Protecting computer systems by implementing proper controls
C. Making is compulsory for employees to sign a none disclosure agreement
D. Categorizing information according to its sensitivity and access rights

QUESTION 33

Contingency planning enables organizations to develop and maintain effective methods to handle emergencies. Every organization will have its own specific requirements that the planning should address. There are five major components of the IT contingency plan, namely supporting information, notification activation, recovery and reconstitution and plan appendices. What is the main purpose of the reconstitution plan?

A. To restore the original site, tests systems to prevent the incident and terminates operations

B. To define the notification procedures, damage assessments and offers the plan activation

C. To provide the introduction and detailed concept of the contingency plan

D. To provide a sequence of recovery activities with the help of recovery procedures

QUESTION 34

The insider risk matrix consists of technical literacy and business process knowledge vectors. Considering the matrix, one can conclude that:

A. If the insider's technical literacy is low and process knowledge is high, the risk posed by the threat will be insignificant.
B. If the insider's technical literacy and process knowledge are high, the risk posed by the threat will be insignificant.
C. If the insider's technical literacy is high and process knowledge is low, the risk posed by the threat will be high.
D. If the insider's technical literacy and process knowledge are high, the risk posed by the threat will be high.

QUESTION 35

Which policy recommends controls for securing and tracking organizational resources:

A. Access control policy
B. Administrative security policy
C. Acceptable use policy
D. Asset control policy

QUESTION 36
Which one of the following is the correct sequence of flow of the stages in an incident response:

A. Containment - Identification - Preparation - Recovery - Follow-up - Eradication
B. Preparation - Identification - Containment - Eradication - Recovery - Follow-upà
C. Eradication - Containment - Identification - Preparation - Recovery - Follow-up
D. Identification - Preparation - Containment - Recovery - Follow-up - Eradication

QUESTION 37
Organizations or incident response teams need to protect the evidence for any future legal actions that may be taken against perpetrators that intentionally attacked the computer system. EVIDENCE PROTECTION is also required to meet legal compliance issues. Which of the following documents helps in protecting evidence from physical or logical damage:

A. Network and host log records
B. Chain-of-Custody
C. Forensic analysis report
D. Chain-of-Precedence

QUESTION 38

Except for some common roles, the roles in an IRT are distinct for every organization. Which among the following is the role played by the Incident Coordinator of an IRT?

A. Links the appropriate technology to the incident to ensure that the foundation's offices are returned to normal operations as quickly as possible

B. Links the groups that are affected by the incidents, such as legal, human resources, different business areas and management

C. Applies the appropriate technology and tries to eradicate and recover from the incidentD. Focuses on the incident and handles it from management and technical point of view

QUESTION 39

The data on the affected system must be backed up so that it can be retrieved if it is damaged during incident response. The system backup can also be used for further investigations of the incident. Identify the stage of the incident response and handling process in which complete backup of the infected system is carried out?

A. Containment

B. Eradication

C. Incident recording

D. Incident investigation

QUESTION 40

In a qualitative risk analysis, risk is calculated in terms of:

A. (Attack Success + Criticality) – (Countermeasures)

B. Asset criticality assessment – (Risks and Associated Risk Levels)

C. Probability of Loss X Loss

D. (Countermeasures + Magnitude of Impact) – (Reports from prior risk assessments)

QUESTION 41

A computer virus hoax is a message warning the recipient of non-existent computer virus. The message is usually a chain e-mail that tells the recipient to forward it to every one they know. Which of the following is **NOT** a symptom of virus hoax message?

A. The message prompts the end user to forward it to his / her e-mail contact list and gain monetary benefits in doing so
B. The message from a known email id is caught by SPAM filters due to change of filter settings
C. The message warns to delete certain files if the user does not take appropriate actionD. The message prompts the user to install Anti-Virus

QUESTION 42

In which of the steps of NIST's risk assessment methodology are the boundary of the IT system, along with the resources and the information that constitute the system identified?

A. Likelihood Determination
B. Control recommendation
C. System characterization
D. Control analysis

QUESTION 43

ADAM, an employee from a multinational company, uses his company's accounts to send e-mails to a third party with their spoofed mail address. How can you categorize this type of account?

A. Inappropriate usage incident
B. Unauthorized access incident
C. Network intrusion incident
D. Denial of Service incident

QUESTION 44

A security policy will take the form of a document or a collection of documents, depending on the situation or usage. It can become a point of reference in case a violation occurs that results in dismissal or other penalty. Which of the following is **NOT** true for a good security policy?

A. It must be enforceable with security tools where appropriate and with sanctions where actual prevention is not technically feasible
B. It must be approved by court of law after verifications of the stated terms and facts
C. It must be implemented through system administration procedures, publishing of acceptable use guide lines or other appropriate methods
D. It must clearly define the areas of responsibilities of the users, administrators and management

QUESTION 45 Incident handling and response steps help you to detect, identify, respond and manage an incident. Which of the following helps in recognizing and separating the infected hosts from the information system?

A. Configuring firewall to default settings
B. Inspecting the process running on the system
C. Browsing particular government websites
D. Sending mails to only group of friends

QUESTION 46
An access control policy authorized a group of users to perform a set of actions on a set of resources. Access to resources is based on necessity and if a particular job role requires the use of those resources. Which of the following is **NOT** a fundamental element of access control policy

A. Action group: group of actions performed by the users on resources
B. Development group: group of persons who develop the policy
C. Resource group: resources controlled by the policy
D. Access group: group of users to which the policy applies

QUESTION 47

Computer viruses are malicious software programs that infect computers and corrupt or delete the data on them. Identify the virus type that specifically infects Microsoft Word files?

A. Micro Virus
B. File Infector
C. Macro Virus
D. Boot Sector virus

QUESTION 48

The type of relationship between CSIRT and its constituency have an impact on the services provided by the CSIRT. Identify the level of the authority that enables members of CSIRT to undertake any necessary actions on behalf of their constituency?

A. Full-level authority
B. Mid-level authority
C. Half-level authority
D. Shared-level authority

QUESTION 49

Digital evidence plays a major role in prosecuting cyber criminals. John is a cyber-crime investigator, is asked to investigate a child pornography case. The personal computer of the criminal in question was confiscated by the county police. Which of the following evidence will lead John in his investigation?

A. SAM file
B. Web serve log
C. Routing table list
D. Web browser history

QUESTION 50

An estimation of the expected losses after an incident helps organization in prioritizing and formulating their incident response. The cost of an incident can be categorized as a tangible and intangible cost. Identify the tangible cost associated with virus outbreak?

A. Loss of goodwill
B. Damage to corporate reputation
C. Psychological damage
D. Lost productivity damage

QUESTION 51

Which of the following incidents are reported under CAT -5 federal agency category?

A. Exercise/ Network Defense Testing
B. Malicious code
C. Scans/ probes/ Attempted Access
D. Denial of Service DoS

QUESTION 52

One of the goals of CSIRT is to manage security problems by taking a certain approach towards the customers' security vulnerabilities and by responding effectively to potential information security incidents. Identify the incident response approach that focuses on developing the infrastructure and security processes before the occurrence or detection of an event or any incident:

A. Interactive approach
B. Introductive approach
C. Proactive approach
D. Qualitative approach

QUESTION 53

A computer forensic investigator must perform a proper investigation to protect digital evidence. During the investigation, an investigator needs to process large amounts of data using a combination of automated and manual methods. Identify the computer forensic process involved:

A. Analysis
B. Preparation
C. Examination
D. Collection

QUESTION 54

Incident management team provides support to all users in the organization that are affected by the threat or attack. The organization's internal auditor is part of the incident response team. Identify one of the responsibilities of the internal auditor as part of the incident response team:

A. Configure information security controls
B. Perform necessary action to block the network traffic from suspected intruder
C. Identify and report security loopholes to the management for necessary actionsD. Coordinate incident containment activities with the information security officer

QUESTION 55

A risk mitigation strategy determines the circumstances under which an action has to be taken to minimize and overcome risks. Identify the risk mitigation strategy that focuses on minimizing the probability of risk and losses by searching for vulnerabilities in the system and appropriate controls:

A. Risk Assumption
B. Research and acknowledgment
C. Risk limitation
D. Risk absorption

QUESTION 56

Based on the some statistics; what is the typical number one top incident?

A. Phishing
B. Policy violation
C. Un-authorized access
D. Malware

QUESTION 57

An adversary attacks the information resources to gain undue advantage is called:

A. Defensive Information Warfare
B. Offensive Information Warfare
C. Electronic Warfare
D. Conventional Warfare

QUESTION 58

An assault on system security that is derived from an intelligent threat is called:

A. Threat Agent
B. Vulnerability
C. Attack
D. Risk

QUESTION 59

The IDS and IPS system logs indicating an unusual deviation from typical network traffic flows; this is called:

A. A Precursor
B. An Indication
C. A Proactive
D. A Reactive

QUESTION 60

The largest number of cyber-attacks are conducted by:

A. Insiders
B. Outsiders
C. Business partners
D. Suppliers

QUESTION 61

The sign of incident that may happen in the future is called:

A. A Precursor
B. An Indication
C. A Proactive
D. A Reactive

QUESTION 62

Incidents such as DDoS that should be handled immediately may be considered as:

A. Level One incident
B. Level Two incident
C. Level Three incident
D. Level Four incident

QUESTION 63

Total cost of disruption of an incident is the sum of

Tangible and Intangible costs
A. Tangible cost only
B. Intangible cost only
C. Level Two and Level Three incidents cost

QUESTION 64

Incident prioritization must be based on:

A. Potential impact
B. Current damage
C. Criticality of affected systems
D. All the above

QUESTION 65
An information security incident is

A. Any real or suspected adverse event in relation to the security of computer systems or networks
B. Any event that disrupts normal today's business functions
C. Any event that breaches the availability of information assets
D. All of the above

QUESTION 66
Which of the following can be considered synonymous:

A. Hazard and Threat
B. Threat and Threat Agent
C. Precaution and countermeasure
D. Vulnerability and Danger

QUESTION 67

If the loss anticipated is greater than the agreed upon threshold; the organization will:
A. Accept the risk
B. Mitigate the risk
C. Accept the risk but after management approval
D. Do nothing

QUESTION 68

A payroll system has a vulnerability that cannot be exploited by current technology. Which of the following is correct about this scenario:

A. The risk must be urgently mitigated
B. The risk must be transferred immediately
C. The risk is not present at this time
D. The risk is accepted

QUESTION 69

Overall Likelihood rating of a Threat to Exploit a Vulnerability is driven by :

A. Threat-source motivation and capability
B. Nature of the vulnerability
C. Existence and effectiveness of the current controls
D. All the above

QUESTION 70

Absorbing minor risks while preparing to respond to major ones is called:

A. Risk Mitigation
B. Risk Transfer
C. Risk Assumption
D. Risk Avoidance

QUESTION 71

The left over risk after implementing a control is called:

A. Residual risk
B. Unaccepted risk
C. Low risk
D. Critical risk

QUESTION 72

Adam calculated the total cost of a control to protect 10,000 $ worth of data as 20,000 $. What do you advise Adam to do?

A. Apply the control
B. Not to apply the control
C. Use qualitative risk assessment
D. Use semi-qualitative risk assessment instead

QUESTION 73

What is correct about Quantitative Risk Analysis:

A. It is Subjective but faster than Qualitative Risk Analysis
B. Easily automated
C. Better than Qualitative Risk Analysis
D. Uses levels and descriptive expressions

QUESTION 74

Which of the following is a risk assessment tool:

A. Nessus
B. Wireshark
C. CRAMM
D. Nmap

QUESTION 75
In NIST risk assessment/ methodology; the process of identifying the boundaries of an IT system along with the resources and information that constitute the system is known as:

A. Asset Identification
B. System characterization
C. Asset valuation
D. System classification

QUESTION 76
Performing Vulnerability Assessment is an example of a:

A. Incident Response
B. Incident Handling
C. Pre-Incident Preparation
D. Post Incident Management

QUESTION 77

The correct sequence of Incident Response and Handling is:

A. Incident Identification, recording, initial response, communication and containment
B. Incident Identification, initial response, communication, recording and containment
C. Incident Identification, communication, recording, initial response and containment
 D. Incident Identification, recording, initial response, containment and communication

QUESTION 78

 Preventing the incident from spreading and limiting the scope of the incident is known as:

A. Incident Eradication
B. Incident Protection
C. Incident Containment
D. Incident Classification

QUESTION 79

What is the best staffing model for an incident response team if current employees' expertise is very low?

A. Fully outsourced

B. Partially outsourced

C. Fully insourced

D. All the above

QUESTION 80

The correct sequence of incident management process is:

A. Prepare, protect, triage, detect and respond

B. Prepare, protect, detect, triage and respond

C. Prepare, detect, protect, triage and respond

D. Prepare, protect, detect, respond and triage

QUESTION 81

Incident response team must adhere to the following:

A. Stay calm and document everything

B. Assess the situation

C. Notify appropriate personnel

D. All the above

QUESTION 82

Which of the following is an incident tracking, reporting and handling tool:

A. CRAMM
B. RTIR
C. NETSTAT
D. EAR/ Pilar

QUESTION 83

Removing or eliminating the root cause of the incident is called:

A. Incident Eradication
B. Incident Protection
C. Incident Containment
D. Incident Classification

QUESTION 84

Which of the following is a correct statement about incident management, handling and response:

A. Incident response is on the functions provided by incident handling

B. Incident handling is on the functions provided by incident response

C. Triage is one of the services provided by incident response

D. Incident response is one of the services provided by triage

QUESTION 85

Incident Response Plan requires

A. Financial and Management support

B. Expert team composition

C. Resources

D. All the above

QUESTION 86

The service organization that provides 24x7 computer security incident response services to any user, company, government agency, or organization is known as:

A. Computer Security Incident Response Team CSIRT
B. Security Operations Center SOC
C. Digital Forensics Examiner
D. Vulnerability Assessor

QUESTION 87

The main feature offered by PGP Desktop Email is:

A. Email service during incidents
B. End-to-end email communications
C. End-to-end secure email service
D. None of the above

QUESTION 88

Which of the following service(s) is provided by the CSIRT:

A. Vulnerability handling
B. Technology watch
C. Development of security tools
D. All the above

QUESTION 89

The role that applies appropriate technology and tries to eradicate and recover from the incident is known as:

A. Incident Manager
B. Incident Analyst
C. Incident Handler
D. Incident coordinator

QUESTION 90

CERT members can provide critical support services to first responders such as:

A. Immediate assistance to victims
B. Consolidated automated service process management platform
C. Organizing spontaneous volunteers at a disaster site
D. A + C

QUESTION 91

The region where the CSIRT is bound to serve and what does it and give service to is known as:

A. Consistency
B. Confidentiality
C. Constituency
D. None of the above

QUESTION 92

The program that helps to train people to be better prepared to respond to emergency situations in their communities is known as:

A. Community Emergency Response Team (CERT)
B. Incident Response Team (IRT)
C. Security Incident Response Team (SIRT)
D. All the above

QUESTION 93

CSIRT can be implemented at:

A. Internal enterprise level
B. National, government and military level
C. Vendor level
D. All the above

QUESTION 94

The typical correct sequence of activities used by CSIRT when handling a case is:

A. Log, inform, maintain contacts, release information, follow up and reporting
B. Log, inform, release information, maintain contacts, follow up and reporting
C. Log, maintain contacts, inform, release information, follow up and reporting
D. Log, maintain contacts, release information, inform, follow up and reporting

QUESTION 95
Common name(s) for CSIRT is(are)

A. Incident Handling Team (IHT)
B. Incident Response Team (IRT)
C. Security Incident Response Team (SIRT)
D. All the above

QUESTION 96

An active vulnerability scanner featuring high speed discovery, configuration auditing, asset profiling, sensitive data discovery, and vulnerability analysis is called:

A. Nessus
B. CyberCop
C. EtherApe
D. nmap

QUESTION 97

The free, open source, TCP/IP protocol analyzer, sniffer and packet capturing utility standard across many industries and educational institutions is known as:

A. Snort
B. Wireshark
C. Cain & Able
D. nmap

QUESTION 98

Installing a password cracking tool, downloading pornography material, sending emails to colleagues which irritates them and hosting unauthorized websites on the company's computer are considered:

A. Network based attacks
B. Unauthorized access attacks
C. Malware attacks
D. Inappropriate usage incidents

QUESTION 99

Changing the web server contents, Accessing the workstation using a false ID and Copying sensitive data without authorization are examples of:

A. DDoS attacks
B. Unauthorized access attacks
C. Malware attacks
D. Social Engineering attacks

QUESTION 100

To respond to DDoS attacks; one of the following strategies can be used:

A. Using additional capacity to absorb attack
B. Identifying none critical services and stopping them
C. Shut down some services until the attack has subsided
D. All the above

QUESTION 101

discovery utility is called:

A. Wireshark
B. Nmap (Network Mapper)
C. Snort
D. SAINT

QUESTION 102

In a DDoS attack, attackers first infect multiple systems, which are then used to attack a particular target directly. Those systems are called:

A. Honey Pots
B. Relays
C. Zombies
D. Handlers

QUESTION 103

The open source TCP/IP network intrusion prevention and detection system (IDS/IPS), uses a rule-driven language, performs real-time traffic analysis and packet logging is known as:

A. Snort
B. Wireshark
C. Nessus
D. SAINT

QUESTION 104

A Malicious code attack using emails is considered as:

A. Malware based attack
B. Email attack
C. Inappropriate usage incident
D. Multiple component attack

QUESTION 105

They type of attack that prevents the authorized users to access networks, systems, or applications by exhausting the network resources and sending illegal requests to an application is known as:

A. Session Hijacking attack

B. Denial of Service attack

C. Man in the Middle attack

D. SQL injection attack

QUESTION 106

A malware code that infects computer files, corrupts or deletes the data in them and requires a host file to propagate is called:

A. Trojan

B. Worm

C. Virus

D. RootKit

QUESTION 107 _____

record(s) user's typing.

A. Spyware

B. adware

C. Virus

D. Malware

QUESTION 108
Which of the following is a characteristic of adware?

A. Gathering information
B. Displaying popups
C. Intimidating users
D. Replicating

QUESTION 107
attach(es) to files

A. adware
B. Spyware
C. Viruses
D. Worms

QUESTION 110
A self-replicating malicious code that does not alter files but resides in active memory and duplicates itself, spreads through the infected network automatically and takes advantage of file or information transport features on the system to travel independently is called:

A. Trojan
B. Worm
C. Virus
D. RootKit

QUESTION 111

A malicious security-breaking code that is disguised as any useful program that installs an executable programs when a file is opened and allows others to control the victim's system is called:

A. Trojan
B. Worm
C. Virus
D. RootKit

QUESTION 112

The message that is received and requires an urgent action and it prompts the recipient to delete certain files or forward it to others is called:

A. An Adware
B. Mail bomb
C. A Virus Hoax
D. Spear Phishing

QUESTION 113

The free utility which quickly scans Systems running Windows OS to find settings that may have been changed by spyware, malware, or other unwanted programs is called:

A. Tripwire
B. HijackThis
C. Stinger
D. F-Secure Anti-virus

QUESTION 114

The Malicious code that is installed on the computer without user's knowledge to acquire information from the user's machine and send it to the attacker who can access it remotely is called:

A. Spyware
B. Logic Bomb
C. Trojan
D. Worm

QUESTION 115

A software application in which advertising banners are displayed while the program is running that delivers ads to display pop-up windows or bars that appears on a computer screen or browser is called:

A. adware (spelled all lower case)
B. Trojan
C. RootKit
D. Virus
E. Worm

QUESTION 116

A Host is infected by worms that propagates through a vulnerable service; the sign(s) of the presence of the worm include:

A. Decrease in network usage
B. Established connection attempts targeted at the vulnerable services
C. System becomes instable or crashes
D. All the above

QUESTION 117

The main difference between viruses and worms is:

A. Worms require a host file to propagate while viruses don't

B. Viruses require a host file to propagate while Worms don't

C. Viruses don't require user interaction; they are self-replicating malware

D. Viruses and worms are common names for the same malware

QUESTION 118

The sign(s) of the presence of malicious code on a host infected by a virus which is delivered via e-mail could be:

A. Antivirus software detects the infected files

B. Increase in the number of e-mails sent and received

C. System files become inaccessible

D. All the above

QUESTION 119

Which of the following is **NOT** one of the common techniques used to detect Insider threats:

A. Spotting an increase in their performance
B. Observing employee tardiness and unexplained absenteeism
C. Observing employee sick leaves
D. Spotting conflicts with supervisors and coworkers

QUESTION 120

Which of the following is **NOT** one of the techniques used to respond to insider threats:

A. Placing malicious users in quarantine network, so that attack cannot be spread
B. Preventing malicious users from accessing unclassified information
C. Disabling the computer systems from network connection
D. Blocking malicious user accounts

QUESTION 121

Authorized users with privileged access who misuse the corporate informational assets and directly affects the confidentiality, integrity, and availability of the assets are known as:

A. Outsider threats
B. Social Engineers
C. Insider threats
D. Zombies

QUESTION 122

Keyloggers do **NOT**:

A. Run in the background
B. Alter system files
C. Secretly records URLs visited in browser, keystrokes, chat conversations, ...etc
D. Send log file to attacker's email or upload it to an ftp server

QUESTION 123

Which is the **incorrect** statement about Anti-keyloggers scanners:

A. Detect already installed Keyloggers in victim machines
B. Run in stealthy mode to record victims online activity
C. Software tools

QUESTION 124

The USB tool (depicted below) that is connected to male USB Keyboard cable and not detected by anti-spyware tools is most likely called:

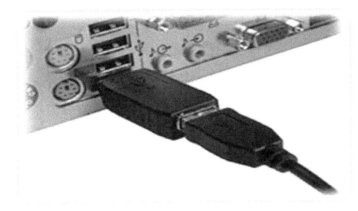

A. Software Key Grabber
B. Hardware Keylogger
C. USB adapter
D. Anti-Keylogger

QUESTION 125

Insiders understand corporate business functions. What is the correct sequence of activities performed by Insiders to damage company assets:

A. Gain privileged access, install malware then activate

B. Install malware, gain privileged access, then activate

C. Gain privileged access, activate and install malware

D. Activate malware, gain privileged access then install malware

QUESTION 126

Spyware tool used to record malicious user's computer activities and keyboard stokes is called:

A. adware
B. Keylogger
C. Rootkit
D. Firewall

QUESTION 127
Insiders may be:

A. Ignorant employees
B. Carless administrators
C. Disgruntled staff members
D. All the above

QUESTION 128

Which of the following may be considered as insider threat(s):

A. An employee having no clashes with supervisors and coworkers
B. Disgruntled system administrators
C. An employee who gets an annual 7% salary raise
D. An employee with an insignificant technical literacy and business process knowledge

QUESTION 129

Lack of forensic readiness may result in:

A. Loss of clients thereby damaging the organization's reputation
B. System downtime
C. Data manipulation, deletion, and theft
D. All the above

QUESTION 130

The state of incident response preparedness that enables an organization to maximize its potential to use digital evidence while minimizing the cost of an investigation is called:

A. Computer Forensics
B. Digital Forensic Analysis
C. Forensic Readiness
D. Digital Forensic Policy

QUESTION 131

Which of the following is **NOT** a digital forensic analysis tool:

A. Access Data FTK
B. EAR/ Pilar
C. Guidance Software EnCase Forensic
D. Helix

QUESTION 132

The Linux command used to make binary copies of computer media and as a disk imaging tool if given a raw disk device as its input is:

A. "dd" command
B. "netstat" command
C. "nslookup" command
D. "find" command

QUESTION 133

What command does a Digital Forensic Examiner use to display the list of all open ports and the associated IP addresses on a victim computer to identify the established connections on it:

A. "arp" command
B. "netstat –an" command
C. "dd" command
D. "ifconfig" command

QUESTION 134

What command does a Digital Forensic Examiner use to display the list of all IP addresses and their associated MAC addresses on a victim computer to identify the machines that were communicating with it:

A. "arp" command
B. "netstat –an" command
C. "dd" command
D. "ifconfig" command

QUESTION 135

The individual who recovers, analyzes, and preserves computer and related materials to be presented as evidence in a court of law and identifies the evidence, estimates the potential impact of the malicious activity on the victim, and assesses the intent and identity of the perpetrator is called:

A. Digital Forensic Examiner
B. Computer Forensic Investigator
C. Computer Hacking Forensic Investigator
D. All the above

QUESTION 136

To recover, analyze, and preserve computer and related materials in such a way that it can be presented as evidence in a court of law and identify the evidence in short time, estimate the potential impact of the malicious activity on the victim, and assess the intent and identity of the perpetrator is known as:

A. Computer Forensics
B. Digital Forensic Analysis
C. Forensic Readiness
D. Digital Forensic Examiner

QUESTION 137

Any information of probative value that is either stored or transmitted in a digital form during a computer crime is called:

A. Digital evidence
B. Computer Emails
C. Digital investigation
D. Digital Forensic Examiner

QUESTION 138
Digital evidence must:

A. Be Authentic, complete and reliable
B. Not prove the attackers actions
C. Be Volatile
D. Cast doubt on the authenticity and veracity of the evidence

QUESTION 139

Which of the following is **NOT** one of the Computer Forensic types:

A. USB Forensics
B. Email Forensics
C. Forensic Archaeology
D. Image Forensics

QUESTION 140

The correct order or sequence of the Computer Forensic processes is:

A. Preparation, analysis, examination, collection, and reporting

B. Preparation, collection, examination, analysis, and reporting

C. Preparation, examination, collection, analysis, and reporting

D. Preparation, analysis, collection, examination, and reporting

QUESTION 141

The person who offers his formal opinion as a testimony about a computer crime incident in the court of law is known as:

A. Expert Witness
B. Incident Analyzer
C. Incident Responder
D. Evidence Documenter

QUESTION 142

Electronic evidence may reside in the following:

A. Data Files
B. Backup tapes
C. Other media sources
D. All the above

QUESTION 143

A methodical series of techniques and procedures for gathering evidence, from computing equipment and various storage devices and digital media, that can be presented in a court of law in a coherent and meaningful format is called:

A. Forensic Analysis
B. Computer Forensics
C. Forensic Readiness
D. Steganalysis

QUESTION 144

Incidents are reported in order to:

A. Provide stronger protection for systems and data
B. Deal properly with legal issues
C. Be prepared for handling future incidents
D. All the above

QUESTION 145

According to US-CERT; if an agency is unable to successfully mitigate a DOS attack it must be reported within:

A. One (1) hour of discovery/detection if the successful attack is still ongoing
B. Two (2) hours of discovery/detection if the successful attack is still ongoing
C. Three (3) hours of discovery/detection if the successful attack is still ongoing
D. Four (4) hours of discovery/detection if the successful attack is still ongoing

QUESTION 146

Agencies do **NOT** report an information security incident is because of:

A. Afraid of negative publicity
B. Have full knowledge about how to handle the attack internally
C. Do not want to pay the additional cost of reporting an incident
D. All the above

QUESTION 147

Incident may be reported using/ by:

A. Phone call
B. Facsimile (Fax)
C. Email or on-line Web form
D. All the above

QUESTION 148

To whom should an information security incident be reported?

A. It should not be reported at all and it is better to resolve it internally
B. Human resources and Legal Department
C. It should be reported according to the incident reporting & handling policy
D. Chief Information Security Officer

QUESTION 149

The process of rebuilding and restoring the computer systems affected by an incident to normal operational stage including all the processes, policies and tools is known as:

A. Incident Management
B. Incident Response
C. Incident Recovery
D. Incident Handling

QUESTION 150

Business Continuity planning includes other plans such as:

A. Incident/disaster recovery plan
B. Business recovery and resumption plans
C. Contingency plan
D. All the above

QUESTION 151

Which test is conducted to determine the incident recovery procedures effectiveness?

A. Live walk-throughs of procedures
B. Scenario testing
C. Department-level test
D. Facility-level test

QUESTION 152

Business Continuity provides a planning methodology that allows continuity in business operations:

A. Before and after a disaster
B. Before a disaster
C. Before, during and after a disaster
D. During and after a disaster

QUESTION 153

The ability of an agency to continue to function even after a disastrous event, accomplished through the deployment of redundant hardware and software, the use of fault tolerant systems, as well as a solid backup and recovery strategy is known as:

A. Business Continuity Plan
B. Business Continuity
C. Disaster Planning
D. Contingency Planning

QUESTION 154
The steps followed to recover computer systems after an incident are:

A. System restoration, validation, operation and monitoring
B. System restoration, operation, validation, and monitoring
C. System monitoring, validation, operation and restoration
D. System validation, restoration, operation and monitoring

QUESTION 155
The policy that defines which set of events needs to be logged in order to capture and review the important data in a timely manner is known as:

A. Audit trail policy
B. Logging policy
C. Documentation policy
D. Evidence Collection policy

QUESTION 156

An information security policy must be:

A. Distributed and communicated
B. Enforceable and Regularly updated
C. Written in simple language
D. All the above

QUESTION 157

The product of intellect that has commercial value and includes copyrights and trademarks is called:

A. Intellectual property
B. Trade secrets
C. Logos
D. Patents

QUESTION 158

The most common type(s) of intellectual property is(are):

A. Copyrights and Trademarks
B. Patents
C. Industrial design rights & Trade secrets
D. All the above

QUESTION 159

Ensuring the integrity, confidentiality and availability of electronic protected health information of a patient is known as:

A. Gramm-Leach-Bliley Act
B. Health Insurance Portability and Privacy Act
C. Social Security Act
D. Sarbanes-Oxley Act

QUESTION 160

According to the Fourth Amendment of USA PATRIOT Act of 2001; if a search does **NOT** violate a person's "reasonable" or "legitimate" expectation of privacy then it is considered:

A. Constitutional/ Legitimate
B. Illegal/ illegitimate
C. Unethical
D. None of the above

QUESTION 161

Bit stream image copy of the digital evidence must be performed in order to:

A. Prevent alteration to the original disk
B. Copy the FAT table
C. Copy all disk sectors including slack space
D. All the above

QUESTION 162

According to the Evidence Preservation policy, a forensic investigator should make at least image copies of the digital evidence.

A. One image copy
B. Two image copies
C. Three image copies
D. Four image copies

QUESTION 163

A living high level document that states in writing a requirement and directions on how an agency plans to protect its information technology assets is called:

A. Information security Policy
B. Information security Procedure
C. Information security Baseline
D. Information security Standard

ANSWERS

1. Correct Answer: A
2. Correct Answer: B
3. Correct Answer: A
4. Correct Answer: A
5. Correct Answer: B
6. Correct Answer: C
7. Correct Answer: D
8. Correct Answer: C
9. Correct Answer: D
10. Correct Answer: B
11. Correct Answer: C
12. Correct Answer: A
13. Correct Answer: A
14. Correct Answer: A
15. Correct Answer: A
16. Correct Answer: D
17. Correct Answer: A
18. Correct Answer: D
19. Correct Answer: D
20. Correct Answer: C
21. Correct Answer: A
22. Correct Answer: D
23. Correct Answer: A
24. Correct Answer: A

25.	Correct Answer: C
26.	Correct Answer: A
27.	Correct Answer: D
28.	Correct Answer: D
29.	Correct Answer: D
30.	Correct Answer: A
31.	Correct Answer: D
32.	Correct Answer: A
33.	Correct Answer: A
34.	Correct Answer: D
35.	Correct Answer: D
36.	Correct Answer: B
37.	Correct Answer: B
38.	Correct Answer: B
39.	Correct Answer: A
40.	Correct Answer: C
41.	Correct Answer: A
42.	Correct Answer: C
43.	Correct Answer: A
44.	Correct Answer: B
45.	Correct Answer: B
46.	Correct Answer: B
47.	Correct Answer: C
48.	Correct Answer: A
49.	Correct Answer: D
50.	Correct Answer: D
51.	Correct Answer: C

52.	Correct Answer: C
53.	Correct Answer: C
54.	Correct Answer: C
55.	Correct Answer: B
56.	Correct Answer: A
57.	Correct Answer: C
58.	Correct Answer: B
59.	Correct Answer: B
60.	Correct Answer: C
61.	Correct Answer: B
62.	Correct Answer: C
63.	Correct Answer: A
64.	Correct Answer: D
65.	Correct Answer: D
66.	Correct Answer: A
67.	Correct Answer: B
68.	Correct Answer: C
69.	Correct Answer: D
70.	Correct Answer: C
71.	Correct Answer: A
72.	Correct Answer: B
73.	Correct Answer: B
74.	Correct Answer: C
75.	Correct Answer: B
76.	Correct Answer: C
77.	Correct Answer: A
78.	Correct Answer: C

79. Correct Answer: A
80. Correct Answer: B
81. Correct Answer: D
82. Correct Answer: B
83. Correct Answer: A
84. Correct Answer: A
85. Correct Answer: D
86. Correct Answer: A
87. Correct Answer: C
88. Correct Answer: D
89. Correct Answer: B
90. Correct Answer: D
91. Correct Answer: C
92. Correct Answer: A
93. Correct Answer: D
94. Correct Answer: A
95. Correct Answer: D
96. Correct Answer: A
97. Correct Answer: B
98. Correct Answer: D
99. Correct Answer: B
100. Correct Answer: D
101. Correct Answer: B
102. Correct Answer: C
103. Correct Answer: A
104. Correct Answer: D
105. Correct Answer: B

106. Correct Answer: C
107. Correct Answer: A
108. Correct Answer: B
109. Correct Answer: C
110. Correct Answer: B
111. Correct Answer: A
112. Correct Answer: C
113. Correct Answer: B
114. Correct Answer: A
115. Correct Answer: A
116. Correct Answer: C
117. Correct Answer: B
118. Correct Answer: D
119. Correct Answer: A
120. Correct Answer: B
121. Correct Answer: C
122. Correct Answer: B
123. Correct Answer: B
124. Correct Answer: B
125. Correct Answer: A
126. Correct Answer: B
127. Correct Answer: D
128. Correct Answer: B
129. Correct Answer: D
130. Correct Answer: C
131. Correct Answer: B
132. Correct Answer: A

133. Correct Answer: B
134. Correct Answer: A
135. Correct Answer: D
136. Correct Answer: B
137. Correct Answer: A
138. Correct Answer: A
139. Correct Answer: C
140. Correct Answer: B
141. Correct Answer: A
142. Correct Answer: D
143. Correct Answer: B
144. Correct Answer: D
145. Correct Answer: B
146. Correct Answer: A
147. Correct Answer: D
148. Correct Answer: C
149. Correct Answer: C
150. Correct Answer: D
151. Correct Answer: A
152. Correct Answer: C
153. Correct Answer: B
154. Correct Answer: A
155. Correct Answer: B
156. Correct Answer: D
157. Correct Answer: A
158. Correct Answer: D
159. Correct Answer: B

160. Correct Answer: A

161. Correct Answer: C

162. Correct Answer: B

163. Correct Answer: A